THE TREATY OF WAITANGI

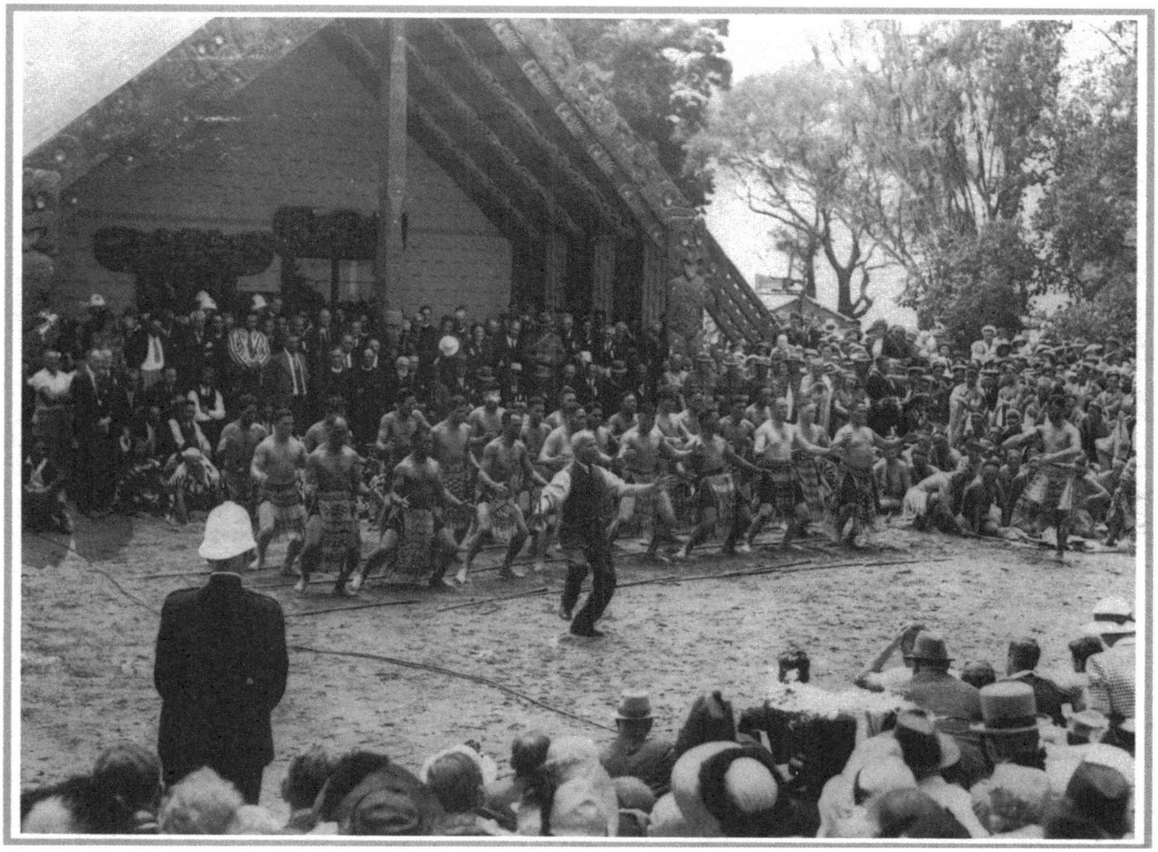

Ross Calman

LiBRO INTERNATIONAL

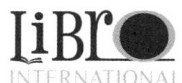

Published by Libro International, an imprint of Oratia Media Ltd, 783 West Coast Road, Oratia, Auckland 0604, New Zealand (www.librointernational.com).

Copyright © 2003, 2011 Ross Calman

The copyright holder asserts his moral rights in the work.

This book is copyright. Except for the purposes of fair reviewing, no part of this publication may be reproduced or transmitted in any form or by any means, whether electronic, digital or mechanical, including photocopying, recording, any digital or computerised format, or any information storage and retrieval system, including by any means via the Internet, without permission in writing from the publisher. Infringers of copyright render themselves liable to prosecution.

The author acknowledges the Alexander Turnbull Library of the National Library of New Zealand/Te Puna Mātauranga o Aotearoa, Archives New Zealand/Te Whare Tohu tuhituhinga o Aotearoa, and the *Northern Advocate* for permission to reproduce the images used here.

Cover: Marcus King (1891–1977), 1938, *The Signing of the Treaty of Waitangi, February 6th, 1840*. (ATL, Ref. G821-2)

ISBN 978-1-877514-34-0
Ebook ISBN 978-1-877514-35-7

First published 2003 by Reed Books
This edition 2011 by Libro International
Reprinted 2012

Printed in New Zealand

Contents

I The Signing

1	The gathering at Waitangi	4
2	The drafting of the treaty	6
3	The treaty is debated	8
4	Thursday, 6 February	10
5	The treaty is taken around the country	12

II Before the Treaty

6	New Zealand is discovered by Europeans	14
7	The arrival of the missionaries	16
8	The British Government intervenes	18

III Since the Treaty Signing

9	Conflict between Māori and the Crown	21
10	War breaks out again	23
11	The treaty in the twentieth century and beyond	26

References and further reading	31
Acknowledgements	32

I – THE SIGNING

1 The gathering at Waitangi

BUSBY'S HOUSE AT WAITANGI.
(ATL, REF. 1/2-030468)

There was a festival atmosphere at Waitangi on that Wednesday in February. British sailors had erected a large marquee made from sails on the green lawn in front of James Busby's house. The marquee was decorated with the multi-coloured flags of many different nations. Great tall-masted sailing ships were anchored in the harbour, among them the Herald, *which had brought Captain William Hobson to the Bay of Islands the week before.*

Sitting on the lawn, groups of European traders and Māori smoked pipes and chatted. There were vendors selling refreshments and a group of policemen from Sydney wearing bright uniforms who had also arrived on the *Herald*. Large waka, each carrying forty paddlers, criss-crossed the bay, one man, the kaituki, standing in the midst of the paddlers calling out the rhythm.

The date was Wednesday, 5 February 1840. The several hundred Māori who had gathered at Waitangi were there at the invitation of Hobson, who had called himself a 'chief of the queen' in the invitation. He had left London in August 1839 with instructions to establish British rule over the 'whole or any parts of New Zealand' that Māori agreed to part with.

The Signing

WILLIAM HOBSON

Hobson was a naval officer and New Zealand's first governor. Born in Waterford, Ireland, in 1792, he joined the Royal Navy before his tenth birthday and served in the wars against France under Napoleon. In the early 1820s he fought against pirates in the West Indies and was promoted to the rank of commander in 1824.

Hobson first visited New Zealand in 1837, following a report from the British Resident James Busby that British subjects were in danger because of widespread tribal wars. After arriving back in England in 1838, Hobson advised that a treaty should be entered into with Māori so that European traders could operate under British protection.

Appointed Lieutenant-Governor, Hobson sailed for New Zealand in August 1839, arriving at Waitangi on 29 January 1840, after a stopover in Sydney. A few months after the treaty was signed, Hobson proclaimed British sovereignty and established Auckland as the capital. He died in 1842, two years after the treaty was signed, and is buried in Grafton Cemetery, Auckland.

JAMES BUSBY

James Busby was the British Resident in New Zealand at the time of the signing of the Treaty of Waitangi. He was born in Edinburgh, Scotland, in 1802 and studied viticulture in France before emigrating to New South Wales with his parents in 1824. Busby returned to England in 1831 and supplied the Colonial Office with various reports about affairs in the colonies, including one about New Zealand. It was this that led to him being appointed British Resident. He arrived at the Bay of Islands in May 1833.

In the time between his arrival and the treaty signing, Busby brought northern Māori leaders together to select a national flag to fly on New Zealand ships and to sign the Declaration of Independence (see page 20).

After the treaty was signed, Busby no longer held an official government position. He continued to live and farm at Waitangi and represented the Bay of Islands on the Auckland Provincial Council. He claimed he was the owner of a large tract of land in Northland and spent much of the latter part of his life trying to prove this. He died during a trip to England for an eye operation in 1871.

2 The drafting of the treaty

In the week since he had arrived in the Bay of Islands, Hobson, with assistance from Busby, had drawn up a treaty in English. In it were three sections or 'articles'. The first stated that Māori would give up 'kāwanatanga' or government to Britain; the second guaranteed Māori continued 'chieftainship' over what they valued; and the third article guaranteed to Māori the rights and privileges of British subjects.

On the night of Tuesday, 4 February, this English version of the treaty had been given to the missionary Henry Williams and his 21-year-old son Edward to translate into Māori. They had only a few hours to write the text that would become the version signed by nearly all the Māori rangatira who signed the treaty. In some places, they had trouble finding Māori words that meant the same as some of the English words.

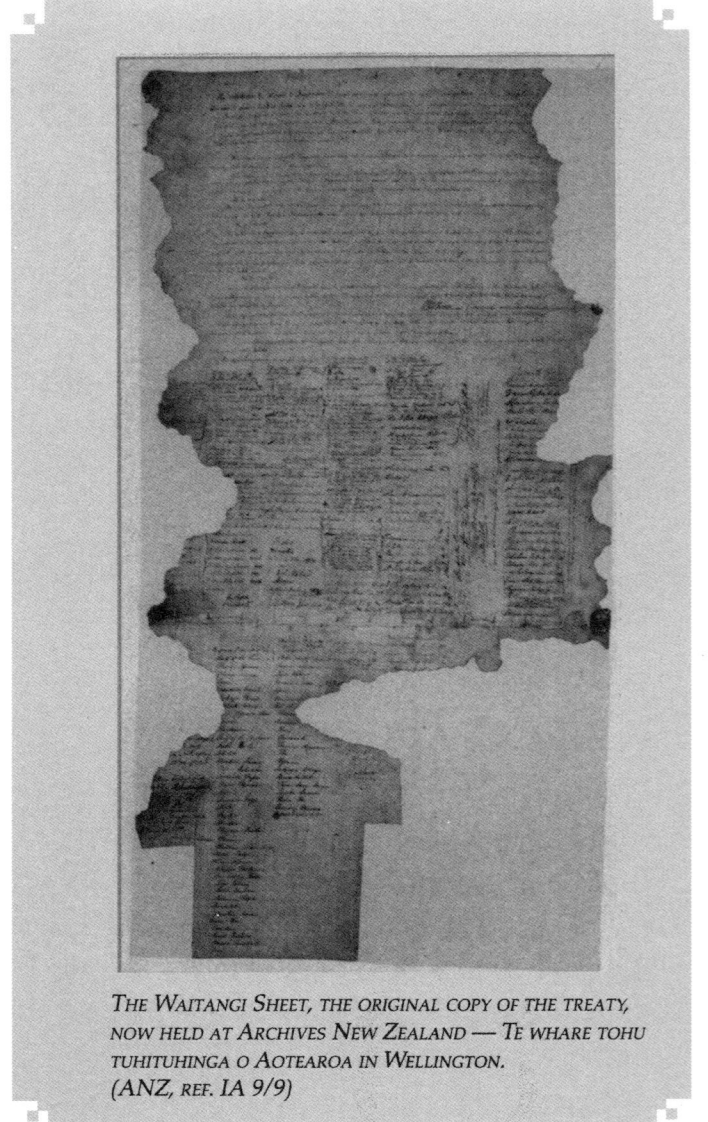

THE WAITANGI SHEET, THE ORIGINAL COPY OF THE TREATY, NOW HELD AT ARCHIVES NEW ZEALAND — TE WHARE TOHU TUHITUHINGA O AOTEAROA IN WELLINGTON. (ANZ, REF. IA 9/9)

The Signing

THE DIFFERENCE BETWEEN THE ENGLISH AND THE MĀORI VERSIONS OF THE TREATY

The difference between the two versions of the treaty has been the source of much debate, which continues to this day. While Pākehā have tended to refer to the English version of the treaty, it is the Māori version that was signed by most of the chiefs. Part of the problem is that some words in the English version, such as 'government', did not have equivalent terms in Māori, so the translators had to make up new words to represent these ideas.

The word they chose for government was 'kāwanatanga', which literally means 'governorship'. At this time Māori had little knowledge of the role of a governor. A concept they were aware of was that of 'rangatiratanga' or chieftainship. The Māori version of the treaty said that Māori would let Britain take over the role of 'governorship' but would let Māori retain their role of 'chieftainship'.

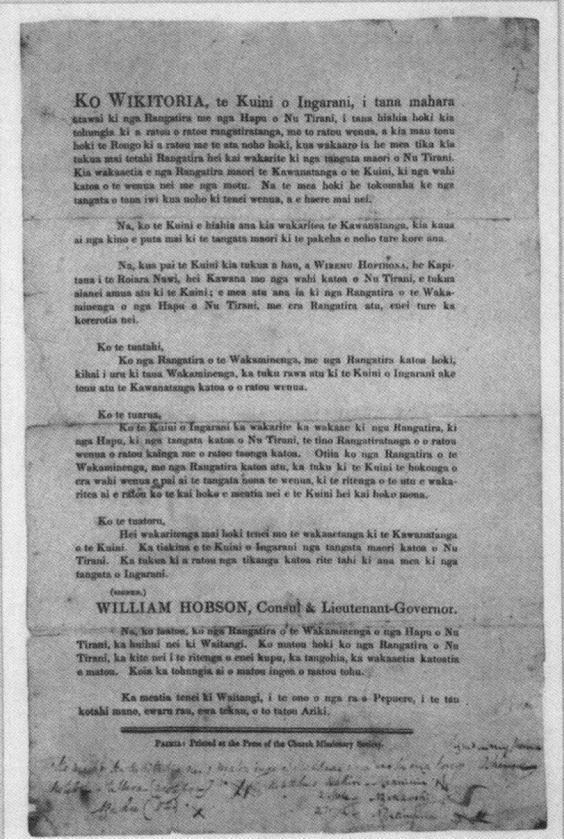

An early printed version of the treaty with signatures.
(ANZ, REF. IA 9/9)

The Signing

3 The treaty is debated

NORTHERN CHIEFS HONE HEKE (LEFT) AND PATUONE. PATUONE GIFTED HOBSON A GREENSTONE MERE AFTER THE SIGNING. (ATL, REF. PUBL-0014-01)

QUEEN VICTORIA. IN THE INVITATION HE SENT TO MĀORI CHIEFS, HOBSON CALLED HIMSELF 'CHIEF OF THE QUEEN'. (ATL, REF. 1/2-055839; F)

Inside the great tent a platform had been built at one end on which was placed a table covered by the Union Jack. Hobson, in full naval uniform, sat on a chair on the stage, surrounded by James Busby and missionaries including Henry Williams, William Colenso and the Catholic Bishop Pompallier. The tent filled rapidly, with Europeans standing around the edge of the tent and Māori sitting on the grass in the middle.

The Māori were brightly dressed in black and white striped dog-skin cloaks and woollen cloaks of different colours. Some wore European clothes and some carried their taiaha. Many of the women wore earrings made of feathers or even whole bird-wings.

Hobson began the meeting by explaining in English, with Henry Williams translating into Māori, that he had been sent by the Queen of England to be the governor of New Zealand. But before this could happen, he said, the chiefs had to agree. He then read out the English version of the treaty followed by Henry Williams, who read out the Māori version.

Following other speeches, the chiefs debated the proposal for about five hours, with many initially speaking against it. It was only the speeches by the northern chiefs Hone Heke, Tamati Waka Nene and Patuone that swung the mood of the meeting in favour of the treaty.

The Signing

NORTHERN LEADERS

Hone Heke and Tamati Waka Nene were long-time associates and supporters of the English missionaries and were at first strongly in favour of the treaty, with Hone Heke the first to sign.

However, Hone Heke soon became disenchanted with British rule. In July 1844 his men chopped down the flagpole carrying the Union Jack at Kororāreka. The flagpole was repaired and cut down three further times as tensions increased between sections of northern Māori and the government. War broke out in the north with Hone Heke and Kawiti leading Māori forces against troops mobilised by Governer FitzRoy. War continued until the Battle of Ruapekapeka in January 1846.

Tamati Waka Nene was, like Hone Heke, a leader of his people who had distinguished himself in war. He had signed the 1835 Declaration of Independence and supported the treaty as a means of establishing order. While he shared some of Hone Heke's concerns following the signing of the treaty, the two leaders fell out after the flagpole was chopped down for the fourth time and Kororāreka was sacked. Nene sided with the government in the war that followed. After the war Nene became an influential government adviser.

Tamati Waka Nene.
(ATL, ref. PA2-2721)

Hone Heke (centre), his wife Hariata (left) and fellow war leader Kawiti.
(ATL, ref. C-012-019)

The Signing

4 Thursday, 6 February

The signing of the Treaty of Waitangi, February 6th, 1840, by Marcus King (1891-1977), 1938. This painting shows the marquee decorated by flags and Hobson in full naval uniform. (ATL, ref. G821-2)

Debate continued well into the night among the Māori who were camped at the mouth of the Waitangi River, near where Te Tii Marae is today. They decided that they didn't want to wait until the Friday, when Hobson had scheduled another meeting. The next day, Thursday, 6 February, they reassembled on Busby's lawn eager to conclude the treaty business and return to their homes.

Hobson, not expecting a meeting that day, arrived after the crowd had been waiting some time, wearing plain clothes apart from his naval officer's hat.

Hobson said that as a meeting had not been scheduled for that day, he would allow those who wanted to sign the treaty to do so but that he didn't want any further discussion. As Henry

The Signing

THE SIGNATURES

At that time, only some Māori had been taught by the missionaries to write their names. Many of the chiefs signed the treaty with a pattern from their facial moko.

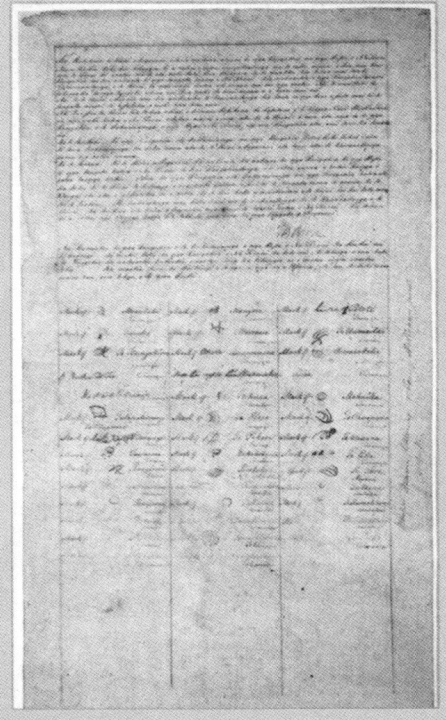

The Tairawhiti/East Coast sheet of the treaty, showing the moko patterns which the chiefs used to sign the treaty. (ANZ, ref. IA 9/9)

Williams read out their names from a list the chiefs, starting with Hone Heke, came forward one by one and signed the treaty. As each chief signed Hobson said a few words in Māori: 'He iwi tahi tātou', or 'We are now one people.' In all 43 chiefs signed. The meeting ended with three cheers from the Māori and the presentation by Patuone of a mere to Hobson. The missionary William Colenso gave each chief who had signed two blankets and a small quantity of tobacco.

5 The treaty is taken around the country

HOBSON'S ARRIVAL AT THE BAY OF ISLANDS AS DEPICTED IN NEW ZEALAND RAILWAYS PUBLICITY.
(ATL, REF. A-109-018)

Over the following days and weeks the treaty was taken to various locations around the country.

Copies of the treaty were signed from Kaitaia in the north to Ruapuke Island (in Foveaux Strait) in the south, with around five hundred signatures in total collected at about fifty hui. The last signatures were collected in September, seven months after the treaty was first signed.

However, a number of very important chiefs did not sign the treaty, including Te Wherowhero of Waikato (later to become the first Māori King), Taraia of Thames and Tupaea of Tauranga. Te Arawa and Ngāti Tūwharetoa also refused to sign. Other iwi in Taranaki and Whanganui did not have the opportunity to sign the treaty because no gatherings were held there. Only a few chiefs from the Hawke's Bay and Wairarapa signed the treaty.

The Signing

THE TREATY AND WOMEN

Te Rangitopeora of Ngāti Toa and Ngāti Raukawa was a famous composer and the niece of Te Rauparaha. She was a leader of her people and fought in battle. She was one of five women to sign the Treaty of Waitangi.

Te Rangitopeora. (ATL, ref. PA2-2808)

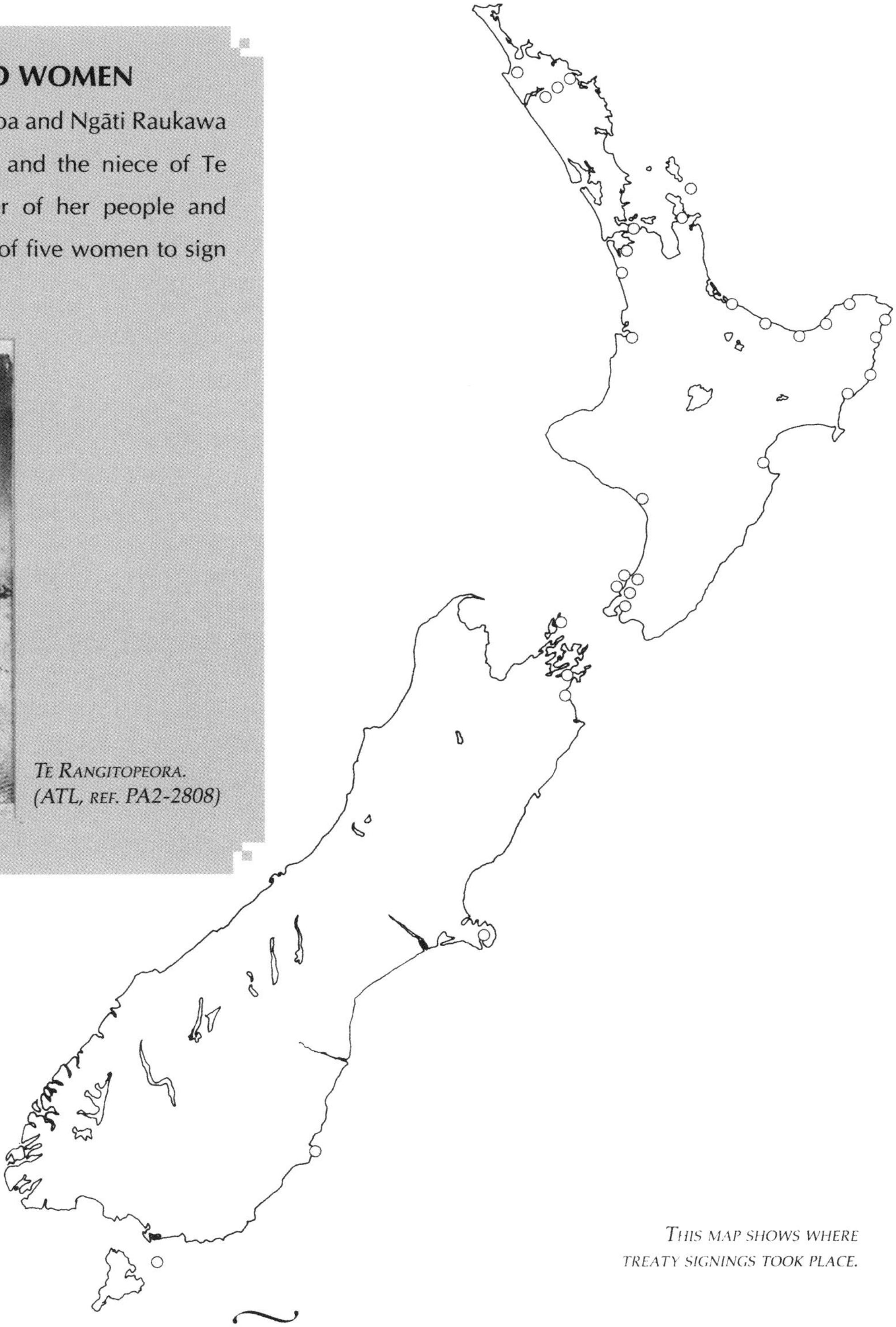

This map shows where treaty signings took place.

II – Before the Treaty

6 New Zealand is discovered by Europeans

Tom Jackson, Tom Norton, Jim Norton and whale, Kaikōura.
(ATL, ref. 1/2 -026954)

In 1840, when the treaty was signed, there were about 2000 Europeans living in New Zealand, scattered around the coast. The largest European settlement was Kororāreka (present-day Russell) in the Bay of Islands, which had a reputation as a lawless frontier town. However, until Captain James Cook re-discovered New Zealand in 1769, Māori had undisturbed possession of the whole country.

Within twenty years of Cook's arrival, Britain had established a colony for transported convicts at Port Jackson in Sydney, Australia. Soon after this sealers and whalers travelled to New Zealand to exploit its natural resources. These men established coastal settlements in New Zealand and they were soon followed by traders and some escaped convicts. These early settlers often became part of Māori society, learning to speak Māori and marrying Māori women.

MEN WITH CLUBBED SEALS, CAMPBELL ISLAND.
(ATL, REF. 1/2-100388)

The relationship between Māori and these early European settlers was mutually beneficial. Māori benefited from the presence of Europeans in their communities through the acquisition of trade goods such as clothing, hardware and guns while the Europeans received natural resources such as flax and food such as pigs and potatoes in return.

7 The arrival of the missionaries

THE FIRST CHRISTIAN CHURCH SERVICE IN NEW ZEALAND WAS CONDUCTED BY SAMUEL MARSDEN AT THE BAY OF ISLANDS IN 1814. (ATL, REF. B-077-006)

The arrival of guns intensified intertribal warfare. This, along with European diseases to which Māori had no natural resistance, meant that many Māori died and others were displaced from their homelands.

In 1814 the first Christian church service was conducted by the visiting Sydney-based missionary, Samuel Marsden. He was followed by missionaries of other denominations, mainly from Britain and France.

Partly due to the violence and hardship produced by warfare and disease, and partly because Christianity had many parallels in traditional Māori religious beliefs, many Māori converted to the new religion and accepted the missionaries as peacemakers in tribal conflicts.

Many Māori language translations of the Bible were printed and literacy, the ability to read and write, spread among Māori. It has been said that literacy was higher among Māori at this time than it was among Europeans, as most schools were run by missionaries.

Missionaries played an important part in the signing of the Treaty of Waitangi. This was due to the fact that they had lived among Māori and were trusted by many Māori leaders.

Before the Treaty

HENRY WILLIAMS

Henry Williams had been in New Zealand since 1823 as a missionary for the Anglican Church Missionary Society. He worked hard to learn the Māori language and gained a lot of respect from Māori, especially those in the north where he lived. He was able to intervene in tribal disputes and later, when European settlers started arriving, he mediated between settlers and Māori. It was largely due to his influence that so many Māori signed the treaty. It was also his imprecise translation that has led to misunderstandings between the two treaty partners ever since.

WILLIAM COLENSO

William Colenso arrived in Paihia, Bay of Islands, in 1834 to run a printing press for the Church Missionary Society. He printed translations from the Bible and prayer books.

At the treaty signing he interrupted proceedings just as Hone Heke was about to sign to ask if the Māori leaders really understood what they were signing. Hobson, annoyed at this interruption, assured Colenso that they did, and the signing went ahead. Later, Colenso published his own account of the treaty signing.

JEAN BAPTISTE FRANÇOIS POMPALLIER

Jean Baptiste François Pompallier was born in Lyons, France, in 1801. He arrived in New Zealand in January 1838, after establishing Catholic mission stations at Wallis and Futuna Islands. At the treaty signing on 6 February, Bishop Pompallier asked Hobson to include a fourth treaty article, which guaranteed religious freedom. While he probably did this so that his own Catholic faith would be respected, the fourth article also guarantees Māori the right to practise their traditional religion.

8 The British Government intervenes

AN ARTIST'S IMPRESSION OF THE NEW ZEALAND COMPANY'S SHIP, THE TORY, ENTERING WELLINGTON HARBOUR.
(ATL, REF. C-033-005)

By the 1830s pressure was building on the British Government to take control over all or part of New Zealand.

Sydney-based traders and investors saw an opportunity to make a lot of money through buying up large tracts of land in New Zealand and by supplying goods to people based in New Zealand at high prices. However, they wanted the British Government to take control of the country to bring an end to warfare and lawlessness, which were not good for business.

Māori and European alike were concerned about the thriving trade in preserved Māori heads and the part played by an English ship's captain in helping Te Rauparaha to ambush and massacre Ngāi Tahu at Akaroa in 1830, by hiding a war party in the hold of his ship, the *Elizabeth*, in return for a quantity of flax.

In 1831, 13 northern chiefs petitioned King William IV of England for protection against a French invasion after a French warship arrived in New Zealand waters.

The Colonial Office in London (the government department responsible for Britain's colonies) appointed James Busby to the post of 'British Resident' in New Zealand. Arriving in May 1833, Busby's job was to protect traders, settlers and Māori. However, without soldiers or a police force he was often powerless to act.

Busby did gather northern Māori chiefs together in 1834 to choose a flag to fly on New Zealand ships and, in 1835, to sign the Declaration of Independence of New Zealand.

William Hobson, who had transported convicts to Australia on the frigate *Rattlesnake* and was involved in the founding of Melbourne, travelled on to New Zealand in 1837 following a letter from Busby expressing concern about intertribal warfare. Hobson spent a month in New Zealand and then wrote a report which he sent to the Colonial Office in London, describing widespread conflict and recommending British intervention.

In May 1839, a private company called the New Zealand Company sent a group of its employees aboard the *Tory* to purchase land for settlers who were to leave England four months later, in September 1839. This forced the British Government into action, as they were concerned that violence might break out between settlers and Māori. They decided to establish a British colony in New Zealand.

Because Britain already recognised New Zealand as an independent country under the 1835 Declaration of Independence, they needed a treaty with Māori in order to take over the government of the country. Hobson left England in August 1839; his task was to get the 'free and intelligent consent' of chiefs to the treaty.

1835 DECLARATION OF INDEPENDENCE

The Declaration of Independence of New Zealand was signed on 28 October 1835 by 34 Māori rangatira who called themselves the Confederation of the United Tribes of Aotearoa. They had been called together by the British Resident James Busby, who was concerned that the eccentric French aristocrat Baron de Thierry was planning to create an independent state in the Hokianga.

The declaration asserted New Zealand's independence under Māori rule. This was one of the reasons that Britain wanted Hobson to sign a treaty with Māori in 1840, because at this time Britain recognised New Zealand as an independent nation.

The first page of the 1835 Declaration of Independence. (ANZ, ref. IA 9/1)

III – Since the Treaty Signing

9 Conflict between Māori and the Crown

Ngāti Toa chief Te Rangihaeata opposed the settlement of the Hutt Valley. (ATL, ref. A-286-014)

Those chiefs who had signed the treaty expected Britain to control the Europeans who lived in New Zealand and to protect Māori from invasion by other countries such as France.

They also expected there to be an increase in trade. However, they had no idea that the country was about to be flooded by European settlers.

The treaty had not long been in place before conflict started occurring between Māori, European settlers and the British Crown, represented by Hobson. Many of the problems arose from attempts by Europeans to buy land without consulting all the Māori owners of that land. Hobson and later governors were under pressure from the New Zealand Company and settlers to acquire land from Māori for European settlement.

An artist's impression of Hone Heke chopping down the flagstaff at Kororāreka.
(ATL, ref. A-004-037)

In 1843 at Wairau (Marlborough), Māori and Europeans were killed following attempts to survey land that Te Rauparaha claimed was still owned by his tribe. Hone Heke, who had been the first to sign the treaty, became dissatisfied with the way the British governed following the treaty. In 1844 he cut down the flagstaff flying the British flag at Kororāreka. This was followed by a series of battles with the British, also involving his relative Kawiti, which culminated in the Battle of Ruapekapeka in January 1846. Te Rangihaeata, Te Rauparaha's nephew, was also opposing British rule in the Hutt Valley at around the same time.

SINCE THE TREATY SIGNING

10 War breaks out again

THE BATTLE OF RANGIAOHIA, WAIKATO, 1864, AS DEPICTED IN A NEWSPAPER OF THE TIME. (ATL, REF. A-109-050)

Māori appeals to the government based on dubious and dishonourable land purchases began when the treaty was less than ten years old.

Matiaha Tiramōrehu presented a petition to the Crown in 1849 that would form the basis of the Ngāi Tahu Claim, which was finally settled in 1997.

By the late 1850s there were as many Europeans in New Zealand as there were Māori, increasing the pressure on Māori to part with land. Opposition among Māori to selling land

This photograph taken inside Tamatekapua meeting house at Rotorua is probably of a land court meeting.
(ATL, ref. 1/2-043266)

was also increasing as they saw the effects of landlessness on iwi and hapū who had sold their land. The establishment of a Māori King in 1858 was largely in opposition to land sales.

In 1860 war broke out in Waitara and continued in Waikato and other areas of the North Island until 1872. Also in 1860, Governor Gore-Browne reaffirmed the government's commitment to the treaty at the Kohimārama Conference in Auckland, which was attended by many chiefs but not by representatives of the Māori King or those then at war with the government in Taranaki.

Following the wars, the attitude of the government and the courts to the treaty was to either criticise it or ignore it completely.

Māori were parted from their land at an increasing rate after the establishment of the Native Land Court in 1865.

Over the following decades, Māori complained that their traditional fishing and other food-gathering rights were being ignored as Europeans plundered these resources or advocated developments such as draining land for farming, which threatened to wipe out whole mahinga kai, or food-gathering areas.

Over these years, Māori presented hundreds of petitions to Parliament asking that their rights be recognised under the treaty, but the government and the courts refused to listen. Following large gatherings at Ōrākei in 1879-81 and at Waitangi in 1881, Māori leaders directed their petitions towards Queen Victoria. To their disappointment she referred the matters back to the New Zealand Government.

In 1890, when New Zealand celebrated its fiftieth anniversary, the treaty signing was ignored; the date of Hobson's arrival at Waitangi, 29 January, became the official anniversary date.

11 The treaty in the twentieth century and beyond

THE TREATY HOUSE HAD FALLEN INTO A STATE OF DISREPAIR BY THE EARLY TWENTIETH CENTURY. (ATL, REF. PA1-O-142-093)

Māori land loss continued well into the twentieth century. The Ratana movement, a religious and political movement, came to prominence in the 1920s under the leadership of T.W. Ratana. Its main aim was to have the treaty ratified as part of the law of the land. Although the movement successfully had its candidates elected to the four Māori seats under the banner of the Labour Party, the treaty remained largely forgotten in official circles.

However, the gifting of Busby's house (now known as the 'Treaty House') to the nation by the Governor-General Lord Bledisloe in 1932 led to renewed interest among Pākehā and Māori alike in the 1840 treaty signings. In 1940, during New Zealand's centenary celebrations, a re-enactment of the treaty signing was held.

The sixth of February officially became

Sir Apirana Ngata leading the haka at the 1940 centenary celebrations.
(ATL, ref. MNZ-2746-1/2)

known as Waitangi Day in 1960 but did not become a public holiday until 1973, when it was renamed New Zealand Day. This name was not popular though and the day was renamed Waitangi Day in 1976.

With this increased public awareness of the treaty signings also came protests from Māori, who called on the government to 'honour the treaty'. In 1975 the Labour Government established the Waitangi Tribunal to hear claims that the treaty was being breached. At that time, they had no power to hear historical claims. In the early 1980s it heard claims by Māori relating to the pollution of their fishing grounds.

In 1985 Ngā Kaiwhakapūmau i te Reo, a Māori language lobby group, asked the tribunal to recommend that Māori be made an official language. In that year too, the government

Waitangi Day protest, 1990.
(Northern Advocate)

empowered the Waitangi Tribunal to hear claims dating back to the signing of the treaty in 1840. From this time, the treaty started being written into law by the government, extending its power.

In the 1990s there were some high-profile settlements of treaty claims, including those of Ngāi Tahu and Tainui. These involved payments and the return of lands, enabling these iwi to develop economically. An apology from the government over its past actions was also given at this time. Negotiations continue today between various other iwi and the Crown.

Debate continues over what the treaty means for New Zealanders today. Beyond dispute now, though, is the treaty's place as the nation's founding document, forged from that coming together of two peoples at Waitangi on 6 February 1840.

The Treaty in English

THE TREATY OF WAITANGI

Her Majesty Victoria Queen of the United Kingdom of Great Britain and Ireland regarding with Her Royal Favor the Native Chiefs and Tribes of New Zealand and anxious to protect their just Rights and Property and to secure to them the enjoyment of Peace and Good Order has deemed it necessary in consequence of the great number of Her Majesty's Subjects who have already settled in New Zealand and the rapid extension of Emigration both from Europe and Australia which is still in progress to constitute and appoint a functionary properly authorized to treat with the Aborigines of New Zealand for the recognition of Her Majesty's sovereign authority over the whole or any part of those islands — Her Majesty therefore being desirous to establish a settled form of Civil Government with a view to avert the evil consequences which must result from the absence of the necessary Laws and Institutions alike to the native population and to Her subjects has been graciously pleased to empower and to authorize me William Hobson a Captain in Her Majesty's Royal Navy Consul and Lieutenant Governor of such parts of New Zealand as may be or hereafter shall be ceded to Her Majesty to invite the confederated and independent Chiefs of New Zealand to concur in the following Articles and Conditions.

Article the first

The Chiefs of the Confederation of the United Tribes of New Zealand and the separate and independent Chiefs who have not become members of the Confederation cede to Her Majesty the Queen of England absolutely and without reservation all the rights and powers of Sovereignty which the said Confederation of Individual Chiefs respectively exercise or possess, or may be supposed to exercise or to possess over their respective Territories as the sole sovereigns thereof.

Article the second

Her Majesty the Queen of England confirms and guarantees to the Chiefs and Tribes of New Zealand and to the respective families and individuals thereof the full exclusive and undisturbed possession of their Lands and Estates Forests Fisheries and other properties which they may collectively or individually possess so long as it is their wish and desire to retain the same in their possession; but the Chiefs of the United Tribes and the individual Chiefs yield to Her Majesty the exclusive right of Preemption over such lands as the proprietors thereof may be disposed to alienate at such prices as may be agreed upon between the respective Proprietors and persons appointed by Her Majesty to treat with them in that behalf.

Article the third

In consideration thereof Her Majesty the Queen of England extends to the Natives of New Zealand Her royal protection and imparts to them all the Rights and Privileges of British Subjects.

[signed] *W. Hobson Lieutenant Governor*

Now therefore We the Chiefs of the Confederation of the United Tribes of New Zealand being assembled in Congress at Victoria in Waitangi and We the Separate and Independent Chiefs of New Zealand claiming authority over the Tribes and Territories which are specified after our respective names, having been made fully to understand the Provisions of the foregoing Treaty, accept and enter into the same in the full spirit and meaning thereof in witness of which we have attached our signatures or marks at the places and the dates respectively specified.

Done at Waitangi this Sixth day of February in the year of Our Lord one thousand eight hundred and forty.

[signed] *The Chiefs of the Confederation*

TE TIRITI O WAITANGI

Ko Wikitoria te Kuini o Ingarani i tana mahara atawai ki nga Rangatira me nga Hapu o Nu Tirani i tana hiahia hoki kia tohungia ki a ratou o ratou rangatiratanga me to ratou wenua, a kia mau tonu hoki te Rongo ki a ratou me te Atanoho hoki kua wakaaro ia he mea tika kia tukua mai tetahi Rangatira — hei kaiwakarite ki nga Tangata maori o Nu Tirani — kia wakaaetia e nga Rangatira maori te Kawanatanga o te Kuini ki nga wahi katoa o te wenua nei me nga motu — na te mea hoki he tokomaha ke nga tangata o tona Iwi kua noho ki tenei wenua, a e haere mai nei.

Na ko te Kuini e hiahia ana kia wakaritea te Kawanatanga kia kaua ai nga kino e puta mai ki te tangata Maori ki te Pakeha e noho ture kore ana.

Na kua pai te Kuini kia tukua ahau a Wiremu Hopihona he Kapitana i te Roiara Nawi hei Kawana mo nga wahi katoa o Nu Tirani e tukua aianei amua atu ki te Kuini, e mea atu ana ia ki nga Rangatira o te wakaminenga o nga hapu o Nu Tirani me era Rangatira atu enei ture ka korerotia nei.

Ko te tuatahi
Ko nga Rangatira o te wakaminenga me nga Rangatira katoa hoki kihai i uru ki taua wakaminenga ka tuku rawa atu ki te Kuini o Ingarani ake tonu atu — te Kawanatanga katoa o o ratou wenua.

Ko te tuarua
Ko te Kuini o Ingarani ka wakarite ka wakaae ki nga Rangatira ki nga hapu — ki nga tangata katoa o Nu Tirani te tino rangatiratanga o o ratou wenua o ratou kainga me o ratou taonga katoa. Otiia ko nga Rangatira o te wakaminenga me nga Rangatira katoa atu ka tuku ki te Kuini te hokonga o era wahi wenua e pai ai te tangata nona te wenua — ki te ritenga o te utu e wakaritea ai e ratou ko te kaihoko e meatia nei e te Kuini hei kaihoko mona.

Ko te tuatoru
Hei wakaritenga mai hoki tenei mo te wakaaetanga ki te Kawanatanga o te Kuini — Ka tiakina e te Kuini o Ingarani nga tangata maori katoa o Nu Tirani ka tukua ki a ratou nga tikanga katoa rite tahi ki ana mea ki nga tangata o Ingarani.

[signed] *W. Hobson Consul & Lieutenant Governor*

Na ko matou ko nga Rangatira o te Wakaminenga o nga hapu o Nu Tirani ka huihui nei ki Waitangi ko matou hoki ko nga Rangatira o Nu Tirani ka kite nei i te ritenga o enei kupu. Ka tangohia ka wakaaetia katoatia e matou, koia ka tohungia ai o matou ingoa o matou tohu.

Ka meatia tenei ki Waitangi i te ono o nga ra o Pepueri i te tau kotahi mano e waru rau e wa tekau o to tatou Ariki.

[signed] *Ko nga rangatira o te Wakaminenga*

References and Further Reading

Archives New Zealand (has information about the treaty documents):
   http://www.archives.govt.nz/holdings/treaty_frame.html
Dictionary of New Zealand Biography (has a lot of information about those who were involved):
   http://www.dnzb.govt.nz/dnzb/
Government New Zealand (has several versions of the full text of the treaty):
   http://www.govt.nz/en/aboutnz/#section1
Ministry for Culture and Heritage, *Dictionary of New Zealand Biography, Volume One (1769-1869)*, Wellington, New Zealand, 1990.
Orange, Claudia, *The Treaty of Waitangi*, Allen & Unwin, Wellington, 1987.
Orange, Claudia, *The Story of a Treaty*, Allen & Unwin, Wellington, 1989.

The original copy of the treaty and other versions signed in other parts of the country are held at Archives New Zealand — Te Whare Tohu Tuhituhinga o Aotearoa in Wellington.

ACKNOWLEDGEMENTS

ANZ = Archives New Zealand — Te Whare Tohu Tuhituhinga o Aotearoa
ATL = Alexander Turnbull Library, National Library of New Zealand — Te Puna Mātauranga o Aotearoa

COVER
Marcus King (1891-1977), 1938, The signing of the Treaty of Waitangi, February 6th, 1840.
(ATL, ref. G821-2)

TITLE PAGE
Apirana Turupa Ngata leading a haka at the 1940 centennial celebrations, Waitangi.
(ATL, ref. MNZ-2746-1/2; F)

PAGE 4
Busby's house at Waitangi.
(ATL, ref. 1/2-030468)

PAGE 5
Left: William Hobson.
(ATL, ref. A-044-002)
Right: James Busby by Richard Read.
(ATL, ref. NON-ATL-P-0065)

PAGE 6
The Waitangi Sheet, the original copy of the treaty, now held at Archives New Zealand — Te Whare Tohu Tuhituhinga o Aotearoa in Wellington.
(ANZ, ref. IA 9/9)

PAGE 7
An early printed version of the treaty with signatures.
(ANZ, ref. IA 9/9)

PAGE 8
Left: Northern chiefs Hone Heke (left) and Patuone. Patuone gifted Hobson a greenstone mere after the signing.
(ATL, ref. PUBL-0014-01)
Right: Queen Victoria. In the invitation he sent to Maōri chiefs, Hobson called himself a 'chief of the queen'.
(ATL, ref. 1/2-055839; F)

PAGE 9
Left: Hone Heke (centre), his wife Hariata (left) and fellow war leader Kawiti.
(ATL, ref. C-012-019)
Right: Tamati Waka Nene.
(ATL, ref. PA2-2721)

PAGE 10
The signing of the Treaty of Waitangi, February 6th, 1840, by Marcus King (1891-1977), 1938. This painting shows the marquee decorated with flags and Hobson in full naval uniform.
(ATL, ref. G821-2)

PAGE 11
A detail from the Tairāwhiti/East Coast sheet of the treaty.
(ANZ, ref. IA 9/9)

PAGE 12
Hobson's arrival at the Bay of Islands as depicted in New Zealand Railways publicity.
(ATL, ref. A-109-018)

PAGE 13
Left: Te Rangitopeora.
(ATL, ref. PA2-2808)
Right: This map shows where treaty signings took place.

PAGE 14
Tom Jackson, Tom Norton, Jim Norton and whale, Kaikōura.
(ATL, ref. 1/2-026954)

PAGE 15
Men with clubbed seals, Campbell Island.
(ATL, ref. 1/2-100388)

PAGE 16
The first Christian church service in New Zealand was conducted by Samuel Marsden at the Bay of Islands in 1814.
(ATL, ref. B-077-006)

PAGE 17
Top: Henry Williams.
(ATL, ref. NON-ATL-P-0020)
Below: William Colenso.
(ATL, ref. 1/2-005208)

PAGE 18
An artist's impression of the New Zealand Company's ship, the Tory, entering Wellington Harbour.
(ATL, ref. C-033-005)

PAGE 20
The first page of the 1835 Declaration of Independence.
(ANZ, ref. IA 9/1)

PAGE 21
Ngāti Toa chief Te Rangihaeata opposed the settlement of the Hutt Valley.
(ATL, ref. A-286-014)

PAGE 22
An artist's impression of Hone Heke chopping down the flagstaff at Kororareka.
(ATL, ref. A-004-037)

PAGE 23
The Battle of Rangiaohia, Waikato, 1864, as depicted in a newspaper of the time.
(ATL, ref. A-109-050)

PAGE 24
This photograph taken inside Tamatekapua meeting house at Rotorua i probably of a land court meeting.
(ATL, ref. 1/2-043266)

PAGE 26
The Treaty House had fallen into a state of disrepair by the early twentieth century.
(ATL, ref. PA1-O-142-093)

PAGE 27
Sir Apirana Ngata leading the haka at the 1940 centenary celebrations.
(ATL, ref. MNZ-2746-1/2)

PAGE 28
Waitangi Day protest, 1990.
(Northern Advocate)